RISEN

Risen

DAILY DEVOTIONS ON THE RESURRECTION FROM THE HYMN, "CHRIST THE LORD IS RISEN TODAY"

Gwendolyn Harmon

Learning Ladyhood Press

Copyright © 2021 by Gwendolyn Harmon

All rights reserved. No part of this book may be reproduced in any manner whatsoever without written permission except in the case of brief quotations embodied in critical articles and reviews.

All Scripture quoted is in the King James Version

Cover photography by Sherrilyn Shaw and Gwendolyn Harmon, used by permission.

First Printing, 2021

Contents

Preface		1
1	Risen Today	5
2	Simultaneous Praises	7
3	Personal Rejoicing	9
4	Resounding Praise	13
5	Our Glorious King	15
6	Death, Stingless	17
7	Once and For All	19
8	Grave, Defeated	21
9	Love's Redeeming Work	23
10	Battle Won	27
11	Forbidden in Vain	31
12	Paradise Opened	34
13	Soaring	36
14	Following our Leader	38
15	Like Him	40
16	Our Inheritance of Victory	43

He is risen, indeed!

Preface

Christ's resurrection was the turning point in history. For Christians, the celebration of Easter, or Resurrection Sunday, is one of the most significant events of the year. However, the celebration lasts just one day, and then we move on with the busyness of life.

The resurrection was a one-time event, but it has present as well as future implications. The doctrine of the resurrection is far deeper than we often assume, and has a bearing on how we live our earthly lives, as well as how we will spend eternity.

Easter is a time when we are naturally drawn to focus on the resurrection of Christ. These devotionals are meant to prolong that focus, while at the same time deepening our understanding of the words to this joyful and triumphant hymn.

Christ the Lord is Risen Today

Christ the Lord is risen today,
Alleluia!
Sons of men and angels say:
Alleluia!
Raise your joys and triumphs high,
Alleluia!
Sing, ye heavens, and earth reply:
Alleluia!

~

Lives again our glorious King,
Alleluia!
Where, O death, is now thy sting?
Alleluia!
Dying once He all doth save,
Alleluia!
Where thy victory, O grave?
Alleluia!

Love's redeeming work is done,
Alleluia!
Fought the fight, the battle won,
Alleluia!
Death in vain forbids Him rise,
Alleluia!
Christ has opened Paradise,
Alleluia!

~

Soar we now where Christ has led,
Alleluia!
Following our exalted Head,
Alleluia!
Made like Him, like Him we rise,
Alleluia!
Ours the cross, the grave, the skies,
Alleluia!

1

Risen Today

"Christ the Lord is risen today,
Alleluia!

On Easter morning, my family has a tradition of greeting one other with "He is risen!" and the reply, "He is risen, indeed!" Many other Christians follow this tradition; and when I was little, it always seemed like some sort of secret code that showed us who "really knew" what Easter was about.

I read once that in the early days of the church, people had a similar greeting they used on Resurrection Sunday: they would say, "Alleluia, the Lord is risen!" This hymn opens with much the same greeting: the proclamation that Christ is risen, followed by "Alleluia!" a jubilant outburst meaning, "Praise ye the Lord!" The word "alleluia" was not in Charles Wesley's original hymn, but was inserted between the lines later on, perhaps with the early church's traditional greeting in mind.

The words of this hymn were written with Charles Wesley's characteristic precision of theological detail. One of those details is found in the first line: notice that Wesley does not say that Christ *has* risen, but that He *is* risen. This of course echoes the wording of the angel's message to the disciples, (Matt. 28:6-7; Mark 16:6; Luke 24:6,34) but it also carries an important theological point: Christ *is* risen. Present tense.

Although the resurrection is a historical fact, it is also a present reality. Romans 8:34 states,

"Who is he that condemneth? It is Christ that died, yea rather, that is risen again, who is even at the right hand of God, who also maketh intercession for us."

For the believer, the significance of the resurrection is not limited to the fact that it *happened*. It extends also to the fact that it *continued*. Christ, having been raised from the dead, is still alive today. Hebrews 7:25 says of Jesus,

"Wherefore He is able also to save them to the uttermost that come unto God by Him, seeing He ever liveth to make intercession for them."

Resurrection Sunday is indeed a time to celebrate that Jesus rose from the dead; but it is also a day to celebrate the fact that Jesus *is still* risen today. He now lives at the right hand of God the Father, interceding on our behalf, and on the behalf of all who will come to God the Father by Him. *(John 14:6)*

How does the present reality of Christ's resurrection encourage you today?

2

Simultaneous Praises

Sons of men and angels say:
Alleluia

In the months between Christmas and Resurrection Sunday, it is easy to forget that the resurrection was preceded by the incarnation. Before Christ could ascend to heaven in victory, He first had to descend to the earth in humility. His birth and life are as much a part of His glorious saving work as His death and resurrection, for if He had not been born as a human and lived sinlessly as a human, He could not have taken the punishment of mankind's sin on Himself.

Philippians 2:6-12 shows the progression from birth, to death, to Christ's exaltation to the right hand of the Father. It also shows us an interesting glimpse of another facet of the resurrection.

"Who, being in the form of God, thought it not robbery to be equal with God: But made Himself of no reputation, and took upon Him the form of a servant, and was made in the likeness of men: and being found in fashion as a man, He humbled Himself, and became obedient unto death, even the death of the cross. Wherefore God hath highly exalted Him, and given Him a name

which is above every name: That at the name of Jesus every knee should bow, of things in heaven, and things in earth, and things under the earth; and that every tongue should confess that Jesus Christ is Lord, to the glory of God the Father."

When Christ rose from the dead, He did something no one else could do, and thus displayed that He is God. One day, everyone in heaven *and* on earth *and* in hell (under the earth) will be finally compelled to admit that fact. We could say that this will be an occasion of simultaneous praises.

But there is another occasion where "Sons of men and angels" will praise God together. In Revelation 5, the four beasts, which are angelic beings, and the twenty-four elders (saved humans) break out in praise to Jesus. Notice who joins in their song:

"And I beheld, and I heard the voice of many angels round about the throne and the beasts and the elders: and the number of them was ten thousand times ten thousand, and thousands of thousands; Saying with a loud voice, Worthy is the Lamb that was slain to receive power, and wisdom, and strength, and honour, and glory, and blessing. And every creature which is in heaven, and on the earth, and under the earth, and such as are in the sea, and all that are in them, heard I saying, Blessing, and honour, and glory, and power, be unto Him that sitteth upon the throne, and unto the Lamb for ever and ever." (vv. 11-13)

This simultaneous praise between earth and heaven is magnificent in scale and will be glorious to hear and to participate in, but the most glorious part will be the truth proclaimed, that Jesus is worthy!

How has Christ shown that He is worthy of your praise?

3

Personal Rejoicing

Raise your joys and triumphs high,
Alleluia!

Have you ever stopped to think about how much Christ's resurrection has benefited you? In 1 Peter 1:3-5, Paul describes several aspects of what the resurrection accomplished for us individually. He says,

"Blessed be the God and Father of our Lord Jesus Christ, which according to His abundant mercy hath begotten us again unto a lively hope by the resurrection of Jesus Christ from the dead, To an inheritance incorruptible, and undefiled, and that fadeth not away, reserved in heaven for you, Who are kept by the power of God through faith unto salvation ready to be revealed in the last time."

First of all, the resurrection brought us new life and a living hope. As Jesus said,

"I am the resurrection, and the life: he that believeth in Me, though he were dead, yet shall he live: And whosoever liveth and believeth in Me shall never die." (John 11:25-26)

In John 10:10, Jesus also tells us that He came not only that we might have life, but that we would have it more abundantly. We who have come to God through the saving work of Christ have been given eternal life.

After all, Jesus Himself said in John 3:16,

"For God so loved the world, that He gave His only begotten Son, that whosoever believeth in Him should not perish, but have everlasting life."

Not only does the resurrection mean we have eternal life in heaven, it also means that we have God's power to help us live in "newness of life" here on earth. Romans 6 explains:

"Now, if we be dead with Christ, we believe that we shall also live with Him: Knowing that Christ being raised from the dead dieth no more; death hath no more dominion over Him. For in that He died, He died unto sin once: but in that He liveth, He liveth unto God. Likewise reckon ye also yourselves to be dead indeed unto sin, but alive unto God through Jesus Christ our Lord. Let not sin therefore reign in your mortal body, that ye should obey it in the lusts thereof. Neither yield ye your members as instruments of unrighteousness unto sin: but yield yourselves unto God, as those that are alive from the dead, and your members as instruments of righteousness unto God. For sin shall not have dominion over you: for ye are not under the law, but under grace."

That's a lengthy passage. If you skimmed through it, go back and read it slowly.

Because of the resurrection, we can count ourselves dead to sin and alive to God. We are free from man's inborn slavery to sin, and we now have the grace of God to empower us to say no to sin and yes to God.

We also have an inheritance, *"incorruptible, and undefiled, and that fadeth not away."* Jesus said, *"In My Father's house there are many mansions: if it were not so, I would have told you. I go to prepare a place for you." (John 14:2)* and in Revelation 21-22 God gives us a glimpse into the grand and glorious place reserved for us.

With so many reasons to praise God for His resurrection and all that it provided you personally, it's no wonder that Wesley calls us to raise our joys and triumphs high!

> ***Which personal benefit of the resurrection most stirs your heart to praise?***

4

Resounding Praise

Sing, ye heavens and earth reply:
Alleluia!

Thinking on the resurrection should stir your heart to a personal response of praise, but that's not where it's meant to stop. Acts 4:19-20 records the response of Peter and John when they were commanded by the Jewish leaders not to speak of Jesus anymore.

"Whether it be right in the sight of God to hearken unto you more than unto God, judge ye. For we cannot but speak the things which we have seen and heard."

They were not just rebelling against an authority: they were obeying God, and they literally couldn't help but speak of the things they had seen and heard since meeting Jesus. This was true of all the disciples, and of the many Christians down through the ages who boldly shared the gospel in the face of disapproval, threat, physical harm or even death.

Just as the disciples were bold to tell an unbelieving world of the resurrection of Christ, whatever the cost, we, too, are to have that same holy boldness, motivated by love and gratefulness to God. 2 Corinthians 5:14-15 says,

"For the love of Christ constraineth us; because we thus judge, that if one died for all, then were all dead: And that He died for all, that they which live should not henceforth live unto themselves, but unto Him which died for them, and rose again."

The joy of the resurrection is meant to be shared. Christ died for all; and those of us who have received the gift of salvation have a responsibility to tell others, that they, too might be saved. 1 Peter 2:9 explains,

"But ye are a chosen generation, a royal priesthood, an holy nation, a peculiar people; that ye should shew forth the praises of Him who hath called you out of darkness into His marvellous light."

As you live in newness of life, saying no to sin and yes to God, not only will others *"see your good works, and glorify your Father in heaven,"* (Matthew 5:16) your heart will also be filled with praise to God. And what do you do when your heart is full? You pour it out, telling everyone you talk to about the wonderful and amazing thing which has filled your heart.

So let your heart reply to the joyful songs of heaven, echoing back the song, yes, but also being the conduit for that same song to be shared with the rest of the world.

Are you overflowing with praise today? With whom does God want you to share your joy?

5

Our Glorious King

Lives again our glorious King,
Alleluia!

The image of Christ on the cross is not what we would call the picture of a glorious king. Instead of luxurious robes, what few plain garments He owned were taken away and gambled over. Instead of a golden crown set with glittering jewels, He wore a crown of thorns, decorated only with drops of His own blood. Instead of an adoring entourage, He was surrounded by jeering crowds. Instead of being protected by faithful bodyguards, He was tortured by Roman executioners. Instead of a throne, He had a cross. Instead of an army, a small clump of sorrowful followers. Instead of the pomp of power, He hung, seemingly helpless and humiliated.

And yet, even though His appearance was marred and disfigured, His identity was not. Above His head was hung a sign proclaiming the truth that this picture of sorrow and shame was indeed *"The King of the Jews." (Luke 23:38)*

The reality of who Jesus is was not changed by the circumstances of His death. Psalm 24:8 says, *"Who is this King of glory? The Lord strong and mighty, the Lord mighty in battle."* The moment Christ looked the most defeated was, in fact, the very moment He won His glorious victory over death and hell. His resurrection is the triumphant declaration of that victory.

Hebrews 1:3 tells us the following about Jesus,

"Who being the brightness of His glory, and the express image of His person, and upholding all things by the word of His power, when He had by Himself purged our sins, sat down on the right hand of the Majesty on high"

With the victory won, Christ resumed His throne as the brightness of the Father's glory, there to reign for ever and ever. When we think of our glorious King reigning in victory over sin and death, our hearts might well echo the words of I Timothy1:7,

"Now, unto the King eternal, immortal, invisible, the only wise God, be honour and glory for ever and ever. Amen."

How does Christ's identity as the glorious King touch your heart today?

6

Death, Stingless

Where, O death, is now thy sting?
Alleluia!

Christ's death and resurrection took away the sting of death. Wesley's words here echo the truths found in 1 Corinthians 15:55-57,

"O death, where is thy sting? O grave, where is thy victory? The sting of death is sin; and the strength of sin is the law. But thanks be to God, which giveth us the victory through our Lord Jesus Christ."

As these verses state, the sting of death is sin. In Romans 3:23 we are reminded that all have sinned, and in Romans 6:23, we find that the wages of sin is death. Christ took our sin on Himself, paying the penalty for sin once and for all and freeing us from its penalty of eternal death in hell. As 1 Peter 2:24 says,

"Who His own self bare our sins in His own body on the tree, that we, being dead to sins, should live unto righteousness: by whose stripes ye were healed."

The sacrifice of Christ on our behalf broke the power of sin to which we had been enslaved, freeing us to serve God instead. As we read a few days ago, Romans 6:8-10 addresses this truth. Just a few verses later, we find the result of this freedom:

"But now being made free from sin, and become servants to God, ye have your fruit unto holiness, and the end everlasting life." (v.22)

That is the practical result of the resurrection for the believer: grace to live holy now, and everlasting life to come. The certainty of everlasting life not only takes the sting out of death, it also takes away its terror. Hebrews 4:14-15 tells us that Jesus came,

"that through death He might destroy him that had the power of death, that is, the devil; And deliver them who through fear of death were all their lifetime subject to bondage."

Because Christ died, we need not fear death. For us, death is merely the instant shift from earth to heaven. Paul expresses the believer's attitude towards death in 2 Corinthians 5:6-8, saying,

"Therefore we are always confident, knowing that, whilst we are at home in the body, we are absent from the Lord: (For we walk by faith, not by sight:) We are confident, I say, and willing rather to be absent from the body, and to be present with the Lord."

We can face sin and death with the confidence that Christ has already defeated them and that we have already been freed from their tyranny to walk in holiness by the power of God.

What does it mean for you that death is stingless?

7

Once and For All

Dying once, He all doth save,
Alleluia!

The book of Hebrews is often said to be written with the theme, "Christ is better." Of the many comparisons made in its 13 chapters, one stands out in particular when I read today's line of Wesley's hymn:

"And every priest standeth daily ministering and offering oftentimes the same sacrifices, which can never take away sins; But this Man, after He had offered one sacrifice for sins for ever, sat down on the right hand of God." (Hebrews 10:11-12)

The priests in the temple offered sacrifices daily. I once heard a preacher point out that the furniture of the temple and the tabernacle didn't include chairs: the priests stood the whole time they ministered.

Jesus, however, offered just one sacrifice, and then *sat down*. He did not need to offer any more sacrifices, because His sacrifice was sufficient for the sin of the whole world. John the Baptist was right when he said,

"Behold, the Lamb of God, which taketh away the sin of the world." (John 1:29)

The priests' sacrifices in the temple had to be made over and over because they never could have taken away sin. In fact, just before the verses we've already looked at, Hebrews 10 explains, *"For it is not possible that the blood of bulls and goats should take away sins." (v.4)* Christ's sacrifice, however, was fully sufficient. Hebrews 9:11-12 says,

"But Christ being come an high priest of good things to come, by a greater and more perfect tabernacle, not made with hands, that is to say, not of this building; Neither by the blood of goats and calves, but by His own blood He entered in once into the holy place, having obtained eternal redemption for us."

There never need be any more sacrifice for sin. It is forever settled, the price of sin paid in full, the debt erased; once and for all. And what is more, the forgiveness bought by the blood of Christ is offered to us freely: all we have to do is accept it.

Have you accepted Christ's offer of forgiveness for your sins? If so, what does it mean for you that Christ's sacrifice never needs to be repeated?

8

Grave, Defeated

Where thy victory, O grave?
Alleluia!

When Christ rose from the dead, He triumphed over death, and His victorious resurrection is the guarantee of our own. For the saved in Christ, this world is just the beginning. 1 Corinthians 15:51-55 speaks of this truth specifically in reference to the rapture:

"Behold, I show you a mystery; we shall not all sleep, but we shall all be changed, In a moment, in the twinkling of an eye, at the last trump: for the trumpet shall sound, and the dead shall be raised incorruptible, and we shall be changed. For this corruptible must put on incorruption, and this mortal must put on immortality, So when this corruptible shall have put on incorruption, and this mortal shall have put on immortality, then shall be brought to pass the saying that is written, Death is swallowed up in victory. O death, where is thy sting? O grave, where is thy victory?"

The day is coming for every believer when we will leave behind this earthly body, being raised with a glorified body. We will be free from our sin nature, free from illness and pain in a perfect body, fit for an eternity in Heaven with our perfect Savior!

Our future resurrection is certain and sure. Earlier in 1 Corinthians, we are told,

"And God hath both raised up the Lord, and will also raise up us by His own power." (6:14)

Our coming resurrection is not based on any works, power, or goodness of our own, but upon the power of God. The same power that raised Christ from the dead will also raise us. God's power is infinite and His promise trustworthy. We can rest in the joy and hope of knowing that one day the trumpet *shall* sound, and we *shall* be raised!

How does the truth that your resurrection does not depend on you encourage your heart today?

9

Love's Redeeming Work

Love's redeeming work is done,
Alleluia!

Two men walked down a road together, talking as they went. A stranger joined them and asked what it was they were discussing. Astonished at the stranger's seeming ignorance of the recent event, one answered,

"Concerning Jesus of Nazareth, which was a prophet mighty in deed and word before God and all the people: And how the chief priests and our rulers delivered Him to be condemned to death, and have crucified Him. But we trusted that it had been He which should have redeemed Israel: and beside all this, to day is the third day since these things were done." (Luke 24:19-21)

They went on to describe how the women had gone to the tomb early that morning, had found the tomb empty, and had seen angels. The stranger, (who was Jesus Himself) replied,

"O fools, and slow of heart to believe all that the prophets have spoken: Ought not Christ to have suffered these things and to enter into His glory?" (v.25-26)

He then started at the beginning of the Scriptures and showed how He had fulfilled the things foretold of the Messiah.

This account of Jesus' conversation with the two bewildered disciples on the road to Emmaus gives us a glimpse of what Christ's disciples expected Him to accomplish. That phrase, *"we trusted that it had been He which should have redeemed Israel,"* conveys all the poignancy of disappointed hopes. Yet, as Jesus went on to show them, their hopes had not been disappointed at all. They were only fulfilled in a different way than the disciples had expected.

Galatians 4:4 tells us, *"But when the fulness of time was come, God sent forth His Son, made of a woman, made under the law, To redeem them that were under the law, that we might receive the adoption of sons."*

Christ came for the purpose of redemption. Titus 2:11-14 is another beautiful description of His redemptive goal:

"Who gave Himself for us, that He might redeem us from all iniquity, and purify unto Himself a peculiar people, zealous of good works." (Titus 2:14)

And how did Christ fulfill this purpose? 1 Peter 1:18-19 tell us in detail:

"Forasmuch as ye know that ye were not redeemed with corruptible things, as silver and gold, from your vain conversation received by tradition from your fathers; But with the precious blood of Christ, as of a lamb without blemish and without spot."

It is the blood of Christ, shed on the cross that redeems us. Christ's resurrection showed that the work of redemption had been fully accomplished. His blood had been shed and accepted as completely sufficient to redeem mankind from the slavery of sin.

What does Christ's redeeming work mean in your life?

10

Battle Won

Fought the fight, the battle won,
Alleluia!

In the garden of Gethsemane, the soldiers came to arrest Jesus. Peter quickly drew his sword and lashed out at one of the men in the crowd, cutting off his ear. Jesus told him to put his sword away, and then healed the man's ear. *(Luke 22:49-51)*

Christ's actions in this scene might not strike us as a good example of a conquering king, but that is because our picture of the enemy is wrong. Colossians 2:13-15 gives us a summary of Christ's victory, as well as what enemy He was fighting:

"And you, being dead in your sins and the uncircumcision of your flesh, hath He quickened together with Him, having forgiven you all trespasses; Blotting out the handwriting of ordinances that was against us, which was contrary to us, and took it out of the way, nailing it to His cross; And having spoiled principalities and powers, He made a shew of them openly, triumphing over them in it."

We tend to view the Jewish religious leaders as the "enemy" of the Easter story, or perhaps Herod, or Pilate, or Judas, or the soldiers. But none of them were Christ's enemy. In fact, His death was as much for them as it was for you and me.

So who was the enemy He conquered? Colossians 2:15 mentions *principalities and powers*. That is how Paul often describes Satan and his demonic forces.

You see, the battle Christ won was spiritual, against a spiritual enemy. We, having been freed from our imprisonment to sin, are now on Christ's side: that means His enemy is now our enemy.

Actually, Satan and his forces have been *our* enemies since the beginning. What has changed is that *we* now choose to be *Satan's* enemy, instead of God's. Ephesians 6:12 reminds us whom we are really fighting:

"For we wrestle not against flesh and blood, but against principalities, against powers, against the rulers of the darkness of this world, against spiritual wickedness in high places."

Christ's victory was over Satan, and it was final. The fate of Satan and his forces has already been determined: and since God is omniscient and eternal, the date of Satan's final imprisonment in hell has already been scheduled. In fact, God tells us what the final chapter looks like for our enemy in the book of Revelation.

"And the devil that deceived them was cast into the lake of fire and brimstone, where the beast and the false prophet are, and shall be tormented day and night for ever and ever." (20:10)

"And death and hell were cast into the lake of fire. This is the second death." (20:14)

Christ has indeed fought the fight, and the battle has been won, once and for all.

Are you living today in the spiritual victory Christ has already won?

11

Forbidden in Vain

Death in vain forbids Him rise,
Alleluia!

This was always my favorite line of Wesley's hymn text. It gives such a triumphantly poetic description of the resurrection. It echoes Peter's words to the crowd in Jerusalem at Pentecost, saying that Jesus,

"being delivered by the determinate counsel and foreknowledge of God, ye have taken, and by wicked hands have crucified and slain: Whom God hath raised up, having loosed the pains of death: because it was not possible that He should be holden of it." (Acts 2:23-24)

Think about that last statement: *"It was not possible that He should be holden of it."*

Christ rose from the dead because death had no power over Him. In the first chapter of Revelation, Jesus makes the triumphant statement:

"I am He that liveth, and was dead; and, behold, I am alive for evermore, Amen; and have the keys of hell and of death." (1:18)

Since death had no power over Christ, it can have no power over us. As the saved in Christ, we are partakers of His resurrection. Jesus Himself declared,

"I am the resurrection, and the life: he that believeth in Me, though he were dead, yet shall he live." (John 11:25)

Do you remember to whom these encouraging words were originally spoken? It was to Martha, whose brother Lazarus had died. Jesus spoke these words just before raising Lazarus to life again.

The amazing thing is, these words are true for us today, as well as for Martha over two thousand years ago. Jesus is still the resurrection and the life. And we who believe in Him, though dead in sins, can still experience *spiritual* resurrection now, as well as *physical* resurrection as we enter eternity with the Lord.

But that's not all.

Jesus had more to say, and the rest of His statement to Martha is just as encouraging:

"And whosoever liveth and believeth in Me shall never die." (v. 26)

When we trust Christ for salvation, our final destination is changed from eternal death to eternal life. But that decision to trust Christ must be made while we are living. Even a moment after death is already too late. That is what makes the gospel message so urgent.

After saying these things to Martha, Jesus asked a question that seems appropriate here as well:

"Believest thou this?"

If we believe that Jesus is indeed the Resurrection and the Life, how can we not share that truth with a world full of people heading towards eternal death?

How does your belief in who Jesus is affect your desire to tell people about Him?

12

Paradise Opened

Christ has opened Paradise,
Alleluia!

There were three crosses on the hill where Christ was crucified. Two thieves were executed there with Him, one on either side. At the beginning of the excruciating process of death, the two thieves both mocked Jesus, but later on, one rebuked the other, saying,

"Dost not thou fear God, seeing thou art in the same condemnation? And we indeed justly; for we receive the due reward of our deeds: but this Man hath done nothing amiss."

Turning to Jesus, the thief said, *"Lord, remember me when Thou comest into Thy kingdom." (Luke 23:41-42)*

Jesus' answer to the thief must have filled him with joy:

"Verily I say unto thee, To day shalt thou be with Me in paradise." (v.43)

Ever wonder about that word *paradise*? The English word only occurs three times in the New Testament, and each time it refers to heaven. In 1 Corinthians 12:4, Paul speaks of "a man" he knew who had been caught up into paradise, perhaps in a vision, but the most enlightening is the third use of the word paradise, found in Revelation 2:7

"He that hath an ear, let him hear what the Spirit saith unto the churches; To him that overcometh will I give to eat of the tree of life, which is in the midst of the paradise of God."

Revelation 22 contains a description of that paradise, also called the New Jerusalem:

"And he showed me a pure river of water of life, clear as crystal, proceeding out of the throne of God and of the Lamb. In the midst of the street of it, and on either side of the river, was there the tree of life..." (vv.1-2)

This fits the description of paradise in Revelation 2, and the passage goes on to tell us a little more about this paradise that Christ has opened:

"And there shall be no more curse: but the throne of God and of the Lamb shall be in it; and His servants shall serve Him: And they shall see His face; and His name shall be in their foreheads. And there shall be no night there; and they need no candle, neither light of the sun; for the Lord God giveth them light: and they shall reign for ever and ever." (vv.3-5)

No night, no darkness, no curse, serving God for ever, able at last to see Him face to face. Christ's death and resurrection flung wide the doors to heaven, calling whosoever will to come in.

What part of paradise are you looking forward to the most?

13

Soaring

Soar we now where Christ has led,
Alleluia

1 Thessalonians 4: 16-17 gives us a few details concerning the rapture, when we shall soar away "where Christ has led."

"For the Lord Himself shall descend from heaven with a shout, with the voice of the archangel, and with the trump of God: and the dead in Christ shall rise first: Then we which are alive and remain shall be caught up together with them in the clouds, to meet the Lord in the air: and so shall we ever be with the Lord."

I think we all would like to be in the generation alive at the moment of the rapture, to be caught up together in the clouds. It would be a most glorious thing to suddenly hear the shout, the voice of the archangel, and the trumpet, and suddenly be soaring to meet Christ in the clouds.

The verses above are followed with the statement, *"Wherefore comfort one another with these words."* The imminent coming of Christ is not just supposed to be something to look forward to; it is also something that is intended to bring us comfort. What greater comfort, when facing the loss of a loved one, than to know you will see them again on that already-glorious day!

But the literal soaring to meet Christ in the clouds is not the only soaring we do. Our hearts can soar with Christ even while our bodies are here on earth. Colossians 3:1-2 says,

"If ye then be risen with Christ, seek those things which are above, where Christ sitteth on the right hand of God. Set your affection on things above, not on things on the earth."

And why should we seek and set our hearts on things above? The following verses explain:

"For ye are dead, and your life is hid with Christ in God. When Christ, who is our life, shall appear, then shall ye also appear with Him in glory." (3-4)

In one sense, we are already "risen with Christ." As we walk in newness of life here on earth, the knowledge that Christ could return at any moment gives us a different perspective. When we look at our lives with Christ's imminent return in mind, we will set our affections on things above.

This world is not our final destination, and we are called to live like heaven is our home.

How can you live like you're bound for heaven today?

14

Following our Leader

Following our exalted Head,
Alleluia!

In the book of Ephesians, Paul tells his fellow-believers in the church at Ephesus that he is praying for them. He prayed that, among other things, they would understand the greatness of God's power,

"Which He wrought in Christ, when He raised Him from the dead, and set Him at His own right hand in the heavenly places, Far above all principality, and power, and might, and dominion, and every name that is named, not only in this world, but also in that which is to come: And hath put all things under His feet, and gave Him to be the head over all things to the church, Which is His body, the fulness of Him that filleth all in all." (1:20-23)

Christ is the head, and we are the body. We are meant to do what Christ commands. In fact, Jesus said,

"If ye love Me, keep my commandments." (John 14:15)

Obedience to Christ is an expression of love, but it is not some grand gesture of an extraordinary devotion: it is merely the natural and appropriate response of a body to its Head.

In Luke 17, Jesus gives the example of a servant's relationship to his master. Of the master He says, *"Doth he thank that servant because he did the things that were commanded him? I trow not." (v.9)* Then He gives the application of the story:

"So likewise ye, when ye shall have done all those things which are commanded you, say, We are unprofitable servants: we have done that which was our duty to do." (v.10)

So how do we obediently follow His leading? 1 Peter 2:21 says,

"For even hereunto were ye called: because Christ also suffered for us, leaving us an example, that ye should follow His steps: Who did no sin, neither was guile found in His mouth: Who, when He was reviled, reviled not again; when He suffered, He threatened not, but committed Himself to Him that judgeth righteously"

We are to follow the example Christ left us: seeking to do His will rather than our own. Following Him means accepting His commands, His leading, his will as our ultimate authority.

How does the Holy Spirit want you to follow in Christ's steps today?

15

Like Him

Made like Him, like Him we rise,
Alleluia!

The verse that comes to mind when I read this phrase is 1 John 3:2.

"Beloved, now are we the sons of God, and it doth not yet appear what we shall be: but we know that, when He shall appear, we shall be like Him; for we shall see Him as He is."

That statement contains two of the greatest hopes of Christianity: that of one day seeing God face to face, and that of one day being *like* Him. Of course, to be *like* God does not mean we will *be* God: our glorified bodies will be sinless, but not omnipresent, omniscient, or omnipotent.

Yet, to be like God, to love what He loves and do what He would do, that is the longing of the heavenward heart. To be able to fellowship with God, uninterrupted and unhindered by sin, that is what we have to look forward to for all eternity.

The next verse shows us the result of a heart looking forward to seeing and becoming like God: *"And every man that hath this hope in him purifieth himself, even as he is pure." (v.3)*

A heart that longs for constant fellowship with God in heaven will be motivated to work to be pure, that nothing would hinder its present fellowship with God. Just as 1 John 3 said, the more we see of God, the more we become like Him. 2 Corinthians 3:18 explains,

"But we all, with open face beholding as in a glass the glory of the Lord, are changed into the same image from glory to glory, even as by the Spirit of the Lord."

In heaven, we will see God face to face and converse with Him freely. For now, it is the Holy Spirit that enables us to grow in godliness. As Peter says at the beginning of his second epistle,

"Grace and peace be multiplied unto you through the knowledge of God, and of Jesus our Lord, According as His divine power hath given unto us all things that pertain unto life and godliness, through the knowledge of Him that hath called us to glory and virtue: Whereby are given unto us exceeding great and precious promises: that by these ye might be partakers of the divine nature, having escaped the corruption that is in the world through lust."

Notice that it is the *divine power* of God which has given us all things that pertain to life and godliness, and that it is the *promises* of God by which we partake of the divine nature and escape the corruption of sin. In other words, the Holy Spirit empowers us according to the promises of God found in His Word.

So how do we become more like God now? By reading God's word and by obeying the Holy Spirit's promptings to do what it says.

As we obey, the Holy Spirit strengthens us to do that which God has commanded. It's a simple thing but difficult to do, because, in order to obey, we must yield our will to God's. That is something our sinful flesh hates to do. However, there is a purpose for the struggle. 2 Corinthians 4:7 says:

"But we have this treasure in earthen vessels, that the excellency of the power may be of God, and not of us."

As we wrestle with our sin nature, we are forced to acknowledge that any Christlikeness that is formed or developed in us is not due to any merit of our own: it is all of grace, accomplished through the power of God.

What steps of obedience is the Holy Spirit prompting you to take towards greater Christlikeness today?

16

Our Inheritance of Victory

Ours the cross, the grave, the skies,
Alleluia!

The resurrection was the culmination of Christ's saving work. In this last triumphant line, Wesley summarizes the inheritance of victory we now enjoy because of Christ's death, burial, and resurrection.

The Cross: The sacrifice of Christ is ours. The blood shed for the forgiveness of sins is freely offered to us. Salvation is a gift; *(Ephesians 2:8)* it is something which we need not and could not earn.

The Grave: This, too, is ours. There was a purpose for the grave, just as there was for the cross. The cross is the symbol for Christ's sacrifice, and the empty grave is the symbol of His victorious resurrection. As the angels declared that resurrection morning: *"He is not here, for He is risen as He said." (Matthew 28:6)* The empty tomb declared that death had been defeated.

The Skies: As the disciples watched Christ ascend into heaven, two angels appeared and said, *"Ye men of Galilee, why stand ye gazing up into heaven? this same Jesus, which is taken up from you into heaven, shall so come in like manner as ye have seen Him go into heaven." (Acts 1:11)*

Christ has ascended into "the skies," but left the sure promise of His return to catch us up together in the clouds to meet Him in the air, to be forevermore in His presence. *(1 Thessalonians 4:17)* The power displayed in the resurrection guarantees us our home in heaven. Truly the "skies" are ours.

In Christ, we are forgiven and justified; and we look forward to that resurrection day when our bodies will be glorified, and we will then be ushered into the presence of God.

How appropriate to respond to these truths with a joyful shout of praise to the Lord:

Alleluia!

www.ingramcontent.com/pod-product-compliance
Lightning Source LLC
Chambersburg PA
CBHW062205100526
44589CB00014B/1968